Small Fiasco

poems by

Ellen Ferguson

Finishing Line Press
Georgetown, Kentucky

Small Fiasco

ACKNOWLEDGMENTS

Most of these poems have been published as 30/30 poems by *Tupelo Press*

Publisher: Leah Maines

Editor: Christen Kincaid

Cover Art: Anna Ferguson

Author Photo: Ellen Ferguson

Cover Design: Elizabeth Maines

Printed in the USA on acid-free paper.
Order online: www.finishinglinepress.com
also available on amazon.com

Author inquiries and mail orders:
Finishing Line Press
P. O. Box 1626
Georgetown, Kentucky 40324
U. S. A.

Table of Contents

For Zoe, Anna, and Nash

The Last City Shall Be First: Maplewood

She comes like a dog after a treat
Or, a lamb to the slaughter

It's breakfast.
A diner in Maplewood.
A man serves it and swoons
(The man swoons. It's a lovely thing to see.)

The check arrives.
"Call me." The check says.
"Please."
There are two free brownies on the check.

How bad can a man be who brings free brownies?
In retrospect she realizes that in Maplewood, there are no free brownies.
It's not even fun anymore.

Not only has he taken the treat
And slaughtered it with his touch,
He's taken breakfast and sullied it
Restaurants
And even Maplewood.

Bangkok, It's

Certainly not where I live.
Apparently where you live.
Fine. Even lovely.

Often I say, "you need to hit me over the head for me to see
anything, preferably with a frying pan."

Morning!
Dogs everywhere, resting at the foot of shrines
Baskets to offer filled with bathroom tissue, Nescafé, and respect
Pomelo dipped in salt, sugar and red pepper.
Quail eggs.

Night!
Boys playing volleyball with their feet.
Motorcycle taxis.
Expats at the blues bar.
Young women. Young, young, young, young women.
People who do not remind me of you
True: they are you now.

A Relatively True Account of Talking to My Son From Fire Island

I called my son on the last night
When I couldn't watch the sun set with you
Because your interest waned: spoiler alert

Usually you insisted on ice cream first
Because that was the way it was done
But on the last night
You did not want any

"My child," I said
"I am coming home from Fire Island."
"Okay," he said.

On the first night, you recognized our waiter,
While the sun set over your shoulder.
This was unusual, because people from our neighborhood
Did not go to Fire Island much.

On the second night, you surprised me
With a ferry ride to another shore
Where the best sunset could be seen
From our table. You made a joke
That was actually funny, like the one you made
In the Hamptons
At the end of everything.

Beaches brought out your hidden humor.
Maybe we should have just stayed on the beach,
Maybe you would not have lost interest
Even in grazing my knee during movies.

When I wrote my dissertation on Frank O'Hara
When I taught Mayakovsky to the youth of New Jersey
No one said this:
Listen while men
Talk to the sun
Because soon, they will tire of talking, even to a ball of fire.
So what more can you expect
When you are not exactly
A ball of fire?

Anna Manhattan

Before the party on Park Avenue
I bought a tiny little dress
Black and white
Geometric.
It was like fitting in a prism
Beside you.
Not the tallest of men,
At the time you sported a cane

Came home
Read your biography
You started as a waiter
And now run a mysterious lab
Creating life
In addition to being French.
French chemist
I will keep you
In my imagination
Where you all end up

Eventually, I helped to create life
We thought to name her Anna Manhattan.
Wish we stole that name
From the family that had it first
Wish I stole you
From the woman who had you next.

Manhattan: better than words or people

Austin is a Young City

"I love you even more than I love Texas." —Slaid Cleaves

Austin, Texas and Athens, Georgia:
Two small music capitols
One eclipsing the other
Each leap year or so

Fly your flag high, Austin
Though Athens has got you now
Parading for Maurice Sendak
Rolling in red dirt and clay

Athens, if I love you more than Texas
Don't tell:
You are younger
And we all know a good swap
Upgrade
Pawnshop
Fling
When we see one.

Ithaca

A photo or two remains:
Girl in sequins
Boy in a tux
After the fire this fall, I gave away the sequins
To Carla: she is young.

Carla and the sequins leave my house; I think these things:
Colette, in *Chèri*, wrote pearls are for women
Whose neck will season them
So too sequins, for one whose neck will shimmer

Sequins floating down Cedar Street
Lift present debris, desiderata of fire and snow.
Come Ithaca, it will all be washed new
If anyone can get there again.

Taughannock Falls
Bed and breakfast
A photo or two remains:
Woman on her wedding night
Bloomsday T-shirt
"yes I said yes I will yes" says the shirt
To the sweeping porch and stair

Fast forward
Stare at the middle of Buttermilk Falls
Count to thirty
Turn to the wall and watch the wall move
Faster than buttermilk
Slower than a Bloody Mary at the Glenwood Pines

"Time," my father sighed, "you old Gypsy man."

Letter to San Francisco

This is that story:
I only knew one person in San Francisco
He was away for the weekend
I took one bus to the beach
Then another

Transferred on the corner, went to the corner store:
Apple juice (a sixpack) and pretzels
Got to the beach
Maybe an hour
Guess what?

No way home.

Spent the return bus fare
That's right: apple juice (a sixpack) and pretzels

How to return?
Walked over to the pay phone
Quarter of a decade ago
When pay phones were a live option.
Stuck my hand in the change slot
Full of change

All the quarters
Carry me home

Day at the beach
Quarters in the slot
Who knew a miracle
Was waiting that day

Ode to the Fifth Street Entrance, Prospect Park

I. *"Brooklyn, Brooklyn take me in."* —The Avett Brothers

We are born of pain, all of us
This: our legacy
For good reason we seek return
To that place we understand most

This is a 9/11 poem
This is a poem of 9/11

Sitting on the sandbox wall
Crippled by exhaustion
All movement pain
Breathing no picnic

Watching you: you are a real firefighter
And the fire pole on the Fifth Street Playground is not a metaphor
You are lifting my child
Her hair red as flame

We all claim our fifteen minutes of fame:
A pilgrimage in September is mine.
They are still looking for you
There is still hope.
I carry a pie
Desperately hang it from your door
As if to say: I was here and it mattered.

On the other side of that door
Rests a bed I slept in many times
On the counter, a blender I spun

Out the back, a blue plastic pool
Where my daughter splashed naked
Who am I?
I was your apartment sitter, Dave Fontana

Your death made you famous
Your wife blossomed into the world
I now teach her voice on the radio
Telling Ira Glass about the White House.

II. "I leave Sisyphus at the foot of the mountain. One always finds
one's burden again." —Albert Camus

We left Brooklyn a year earlier
Unable to climb four flights
Crippled by the rent
But you? Not only did you stay
You went back into Manhattan
You returned
Up
the
stairs
Into the flames

Why do we all return
To an infinite stairwell of pain?
Is it because we recognize the climb?

Camus said Sisyphus' burden
Is not the climb but consciousness of the task.
I disagree, Camus
Yet I will test your hypothesis:
When I fall under hypnosis Wednesday at five behind door 211
I will jettison consciousness and see:
Turning the curve of the footpath
Pushing two children, carrying one
Through the Fifth Street Entrance
Back to the fire pole red as Waldo.

Sestina Approaching Newark Airport All Morning

(after Philip Levine, Poem Circling Hamtramck, Michigan
All Night in Search of You)

Most moments, she is entirely, utterly alone
Particularly at moments meant to—
She watches herself float away her three
Suspended from the ceiling for ...
On the wall, the clock strikes five
She was reading the poem "Now We Are Six"

Spring is here! Outside #406!
Let's think of happier times, at least one
Perennials show in groups of five
(How many weeks till the wedding? Two?)
Planted extravagantly, she couldn't affor-
On the wall, the clock strikes three.

They always knew they wanted three
They are two years apart: the eldest is six
Her sister's now four
(Level the yard! See her gardens undone.)
And he's turning two
His birthday treasure hunt starts at five

How many candles? I don't know, five?
The most that he can blow out will be three
The goal, of course, to
Avert bad luck. He must get them all. In the county of Essex
It matters a ton
Otherwise, what's it all for?

It was Prospect Park where the oldest turned four
Her first backyard party was when she turned five
That may have been her Mom's favorite one
The last combined April; Anna turning three
Russian dancers; clowns twisting balloons into sixes
And flourless chocolate cake. It's Passover, too.

Now in his yard there's not one bear but two
Kissing, of course—that's what ceramic bears are for.
(How many tiers on that wedding cake, six?)
Their son's his best man; his toast is at five
She's in her own yard now, seeding perennials for three:
What's done cannot be undone.

Why wait until six? Today, she'll only plant two
Her new neighbors watch her alone. It gets cold around four.
Cocktails are at five; she'll toast each of her three.

Sestina for Wes Anderson

Just returned from a brief stay at The Grand Budapest Hotel
Let's just say it was no Moonrise Kingdom
Not sure of the difference between Tenenbaum's elevator operator and
A Lobby Boy
But somewhere a man who knows and knows well
Plans and schemes to take over the world cake by cake

I expected Owen Wilson to serve me some cake
I thought Bill Murray might run the hotel
I don't know the Royal Tenenbaums well
But I weep and fast at the foot of Moonrise Kingdom
In my house lives the ultimate Lobby Boy
(So my house is not really for children, and

Yet it is full of them every day and
I serve them all their hot dogs and cake).
Michael Chabon in his piece "Wes Anderson's Worlds," boy
He nailed it by calling them Cornell boxes. This hotel
Is the ultimate box, even more than in Kingdom
Anderson crafted a world in a box, well

Certainly deeper than any well
Wider than any church door, and
Vaster than any kingdom
And the icing on the cake
Is that once you walk into this grand old hotel
There is finally a narrator who is not cloying. This boy

Who tells the story is just the right boy
He tells it so well, not just right, truly well
You'll think of Mohonk, or any hotel
Where stories abide; like Jack types in *The Shining* and
The *Streetcar* scene with the birthday cake
Nietzsche's order and chaos collide in this kingdom

But you never forget that it is a true kingdom
This is not so for Jack's labyrinth boy
Navigating that hotel's no piece of cake
It's not that he doesn't do it well
It's just there's no joy, and in And
erson's world, there is nothing but joy, this hotel

Makes me long for boxed cake, there's Oz in their kingdom
But less scary, this hotel makes me love this boy
Who tells his story so well, with no but, if, or and

Francis Underwood and Samuel Beckett Go to Breakfast in Dublin: A Villanelle

> *"They talk while I sit quietly and imagine their lightly salted faces frying in a skillet."*—Francis Underwood, *House of Cards*
> *"And yet you know our covenant: no communication of dreams on any account."*—Samuel Beckett, *Mercier and Camier*

Let's sit and watch their salted faces fry
This is my town, Frank: let's go for a stroll
That's Leo Bloom, Sam—I don't want to try

The actors at the Abbey are quite spry
We'll leave the pub and get a buttered roll
Let's sit and watch their salted faces fry

The bridge over the Liffey burst, but why?
It's not like underneath there's still a troll
That's Leo Bloom, Sam—I don't want to try

Frank, I'd never guess that you were shy
You've come to Ireland to eat oats in a bowl?
Let's sit and watch their salted faces fry

Once I'd drink tea all day under that sky
But these days Dublin's folk all play a role;
That's Leo Bloom, Sam—I don't want to try

"Old Ireland's dead and gone" Yeats said, oh my
But I'll not sit and dream; those dreams I stole
Let's sit and watch their salted faces fry
That's Leo Bloom, Sam—I don't want to try.

Pantoum of a Great Depression

"Our lives avoided tragedy/Simply by going on and on"
—Donald Justice, *"Pantoum of the Great Depression"*

The new therapist said, "Any questions?"
I asked, "Did you study in Ann Arbor?"
"Have you seen *The Five-Year Engagement*? "
"Do you know the iced tea at Zingermans?"

I asked, "Did you study in Ann Arbor?"
He looked at me rather slowly
"Do you know the iced tea at Zingermans?"
He seemed unduly concerned

He looked at me rather slowly
"It's filmed in Ann Arbor, you know"
He seemed unduly concerned
"It's the best iced tea. And the free refills!"

"It's filmed in Ann Arbor, you know"
Dr. W furrowed his brow
"It's the best iced tea. And the free refills!"
There would be no turning back now

Dr. W furrowed his brow
Why pursue benefits out of network?
There would be no turning back now
His cancellation policy bored me.

Why pursue benefits out of network?
"Who's your favorite existentialist?"
His cancellation policy bored me.
"How does fair differ from not-unfair?"

"Who's your favorite existentialist?"
"What will happen in the Ukraine?"
"How does fair differ from not-unfair?"
"Are order and chaos the same?"

"What will happen in the Ukraine?"
He asked if I had any questions.
"Are order and chaos the same?"
He seemed unduly concerned.

As Far Back As

As far back as camp, Russ said "Just feel"
As far back as two, I know I tried
I sit and watch a Super-8 unreel
A red pail and a shovel by low tide

If ever there were a dichotomy
The thinking/feeling one is no surprise
I have a deep and buried memory
Of trying to bridge distance with my eyes

But now I watch as pictures animate
From Kodachromes too vivid, edged in white
Apparently it never is too late
To peel a Polaroid and feign delight

The true surprise is when, despite the fears
The photo comes to life, traveling past years

Ides Eve, New Orleans

It's the eve of the ides
Not really a holiday, you say?

I beg to differ.
Remember when Daisy said,
"We should plan something for the longest day"?

Well, I have planned something for our un-holiday
Tonight, something big!
First, I will get the oil changed on my car
Then, I will get my nails painted green

For St. Patrick's Day, which is just around the corner
Same day, in fact, as the Purimspiel
Which requires three-cornered cookies
With Irish breakfast tea,
Bangers and mashed

With my green nails I will meet the people
Who plan to celebrate with me—
These are people who know Shakespeare
And have not only taught Caesar but Othello!
I may buy rosemary
And candied ginger

Withdraw them from my pocket, and toss them in my bourbon
As if to say, I simply cannot imbibe without them.
We will toast the town
And everyone else who has ever been silly in it
Then we will look at our watches and say,
"My goodness, we are in New Orleans
For heaven's sake, and it's the eve of the ides!"

Everyone else cares about Mardi Gras
Yes, it was last Tuesday
But the flights are awfully high then,
And besides, we don't care. So, we sidle over to
The bookstore, and touch Tennessee Williams' passport
For good luck
Over on the corner, Spike Lee is filming a puddle
Blanche DuBois blinks back the sun

The poet Richard Katrovas is eating a po' boy
Catfish, I think
Alice Dunbar's Praline Woman drinks coffee with chicory
And it certainly doesn't feel as if anything bad
Will happen tomorrow.
This is how it is, I guess:
The wind blows without warning
We eat prawns and drink bourbon
Someone else worries for us,
Perhaps Spike.
So do all the tomorrows come,
Without notice—
Inauspicious arrivals on the wings of numbers
Counted while the Tchoupitoulas dance.

Three Visits to Quebec

First, my parents honeymooned at the Chateau Frontenac
Then, we honeymooned at the Chateau Frontenac
Then, we celebrated my fortieth at the Chateau Frontenac

The other day Anna said, "Why don't we do anything spontaneous anymore, like
Wake up in the morning and drive to Canada?"
I don't know, Anna.

But tonight, I was thinking
Since we are celebrating three holidays this weekend,
I'd craft a trio of New Orleans treats:
King's Cake, Pralines, and Bread Pudding with Whiskey Sauce.

We may not go anywhere
And I may not even have a plastic baby to stash inside the cake
So I will hide Lego, the true sous-chef's partner in crime.
Actually the oven is broken
So I will use my best lemon yellow, lilac, and mint green shades
To frost a Sara Lee Pound Cake.

Allons-y! There must be a stovetop bread pudding
If not, we'll just invent one
I love pralines, don't you?
If I can't figure out how to make them, we'll
Scoop sugared butter from our fingers
Make a quick Cajun sandwich sauce
Tie up the shrimp boat
And serve.

Truly, I am sorry we never travel
But not really
Fried from flying this way and that in my mind
It's all I can do to unpack
The spatula
Untwist the twist ties
And dine al fresco
En plein air
With you

Sunday in the Valley/I Have These Things to Say about Your Screenplay

"Every Sunday should be like this." —Arthur Miller

1. You spelled the word "vial" wrong.

2. It's electric.

3. Both are true: it made my heart race and it made grading Macbeth papers difficult.

I did not appreciate this.

4. The title is an elegant variation on being at a crossroads.

5. Loved the familiar landscape and the literature on the shelf.

6. The end has a great and necessary gender twist. Better music, please!

7. Definitely Jennifer Lawrence.

8. It was fun talking to you about the meaning of the number nine.

9. The chocolate roses were a nice touch. But the rye toast was sublime.

Silhouettes by the Mississippi

Few photographs
Memory fades in and out
Vast and mighty river
Rotund man shadowed like a cameo

To live by the Mississippi
For three important years
Is to sacrifice the exterior
And wire a pacemaker to her soul

Go with her now
Do you have her hand?
See over there? She is reading about the Mississippi
She came here to read about the river
They pay her money to read about the river, and then to think

Those must be some pretty worthy thoughts she is thinking, eh?
Let's listen close:
"Dad, he said he wants to move to my hair"—
Silence
Paternal silence
The loudest silence in the world

See the girl walking up the stairwell,
Past her father who will not acknowledge her
Who is pretending she does not exist?
Fast forward to the end:
Now the silence is even louder.
Lacking visual confirmation, across a telephone wire:
Is she even there?

No brush on the stairwell
No proof
No witness
Perhaps she is only an idea of herself

In a grand weltschmerz of recognition
She turns within to confirm her existence
This takes perspicacity, wit, and a mighty river of intellect
John Donne was right: in withholding sleep
God won. Without *this jewel*—rest—
Only God remains.
Enough for any internal landscape, for sure—
But to witness His gifts
To live in His world and see it
To do anything and to remember it
Dear Lord, let her sleep, just once in this life.

Two Moments

I.

"Understand that; here I am dead now, but look here, what if—
that is, perhaps it can't be so—but I say what if I'm not dead, what
if I get up, do you hear? What would happen then?"
—Fyodor Dostoevsky

Today my son asked,
"What was it like when you died for that minute,
And they had to resuscitate you?"
I told him about the roller coaster.
He said at least I didn't go to Hell.

I am glad I'm back
It was great to spend that moment with you
One moment is moment enough
To come back for

II.

"May your sky be clear, may your sweet smile be bright and
untroubled, and may you be blessed for that moment of blissful
happiness which you gave to another, lonely and grateful heart!
My God, a whole moment of happiness! Is that too little for the
whole of a man's life?"—Fyodor Dostoevsky

In general
A moment is enough
Worth the return trip
Worth the stay; yet
I can't help wanting more
Like that one
Forgive my avarice.
It's one of the seven deadly sins.
Next time I go they may have me down
For more than a roller coaster ride.

Austin, Brooklyn, Summit

At first it was charming
Naming pets after children's hometowns:
Austin
Brooklyn
Summit
Austin and Brooklyn the cats
Summit the dog
Now we have none of those pets
And the children are leaving, too—
Had we followed the animals
As we might have
We would have been forewarned:
So we are born, so do we leave
Austin and Brooklyn to Germany
Summit to a lake upstate
All better off
Without us

In the natural order of things
We are born, we live, we die
So too do we assume positions:
You the animal: follow me
You the child: obey
Sliding into submission,
Dominance, and the rest—
Let's pose the question thusly:
In the event we subvert the order
The natural order of things
Who's to know or care?
We all submit eventually
To authority from somewhere.
Cancel that help desk call:
Why mend what isn't broken?

Wolfeboro, New Hampshire

> *"A man with the door closed is a man working. A woman with the door closed is a woman available."*
> —Attributed to Virginia Woolf

Yes, Virginia, but what if there is no door?
In Wolfeboro, New Hampshire
We sleep in tents
Or on the beach
Once, in a truck
But not behind a door

Who wouldn't envy the girl from Yonkers out in the wild,
Like a fixture from the Fresh Air Fund?
It's all nourishment to her: air, water, cool breezes at night off the lake
Summer as it was meant to be:
All work
No play
No doors
In the outdoors
We are out of doors
Nothing to close or open
No excuses
Every field a landscape of productivity
Where we can work and work and work
Until the sun rises on us
Never having to stop
Hide
Or go to bed

Ellen Ferguson wrote the "Diversity in the News" column for McSweeney's *Internet Tendency*. She has published her work in *Kugelmass, the Journal of Literary Humor*, and recently was a 30/30 poet for *Tupelo Press*, publishing 30 poems in a month. In her younger and more vulnerable years she worked for *The New Yorker Magazine* and *SPY*. Her co-authored screenplay "Demo Queen" was a semi-finalist in humor in the Screenplay Festival. She is the author of the book *Can Creativity Be Taught?*

www.ingramcontent.com/pod-product-compliance
Lightning Source LLC
LaVergne TN
LVHW091234080426
835509LV00009B/1284